Doubting Descartes' Elbow

To
Nicole

"those small gestures
on the big stage."

J

Doubting Descartes' Elbow

JOE ARCHER

The Choir Press

First published in the United Kingdom in 2023 by

The Choir Press

ISBN 978-1-78963-366-5

Contents

PART ONE

cah there was indeed,

somethin unholy, to the unrolling of these scenes

Cast

The Artist.

The Philosopher.

The Muse.

The Reader.

City

All three of them live in the city.

The Artist tries to get under it.
The Philosopher over it.
The Muse gets everywhere.
She has the keys to the city.

They all have a job to do:

The Artist is to blow it all up.
The Philosopher shrink it all down.
The Muse doesn't have to do a thing.
She doesn't lift a finger.

The Artist is do and not think.
The Philosopher think and not do.
The Muse does whatever she wants.
She drives with the wind in her hair.

The Artist looks to the future.
The Philosopher to the past.
The Muse looks neither way as she crosses the street.
She can see with both ears.

Overall:

The Muse sits idly/ideally by and waits while The Artist and The Philosopher team-up and say something like this:

"as the
feeling
f
a
l
l
s
the
form
appears."

ya feel me

Rationality.

On returning to.

Eagle-eye view.

Atop the Ferris Wheel:

down there, in the past

overlooking the city

an exploding galaxy of undeceiving light.

Seeing it all for as it is.

was

Brick-by-slow-brick; in microscopic, devilish detail – for He always in there, read him between the lines and among the streets, anticlockwise around dem castle walls.

housekeeping

Before we open up a world, gonna lay here and drop down deep, eye-close darkness as we go swim in and fish out. Like adjusting the frequency to the crackling of overlapping sounds, ancient voices, through these falling layers and levels of the city's gutty underworld – of rumblings and murmurs and vibrations and chattering, eventually managing to touch other minds on the way out-in, these clear diamonds, flashes of snapshot memories, faces, and of future things, all that bright geography out there and dark oceans of landscape in here.

This happen as I make these words.

And turn a page.

Kant

can.

He barely left his own city.
He did most of his travelling indoors.

Although apparently he gave banging dinner parties.

Liked to gossip and dance and flirt and was a belter at the old karaoke. Mostly big 70's/80's numbers from bands like the Eagles, REO Speedwagon, AC/DC and the Mac.

Big Love, Little Lies, were among his favourites.

His night had tango in it.

He hated lying and was kind of famous for that.

Outside of his dinner parties he had a serious head for business.

Work hard, play hard, would have been his motto.

him and us

Cnut vs Kant cah the truth and the telling of it has to be the highest form of rationality. If you think about It. If you stop and sit and really think about it for real.

If you take it all the way to the end of the line.

big lies, little love

Rationality is . . . sayin what happen.

Highest form of courage too.

Cept for a few extreme circumstances, being truthful, telling the truth or what you know to be your truth, is as rational as there is. Why would we want anything else, anything less than?

As someone who done gone work with energy, like You do, she must just know how poisonous that lying is. Hunts and haunts and hangs and harms everything it touches and lives in. *In.* It gets in everywhere and wreaks havoc, shuts all systems down. Slow, malignant, eventual.

Read the small print:

quick fix with guaranteed long-term damage.

Buy now, pay later.

It changes the past and sets up a crueller version of the future.

Takes the piss out of it all.

Makes us non-people.

Shakes the foundations until the bottom-end of the world falls through.

As my man says, "a royal road to chaos."

Class

act.

Athens

and the

Academy of Recycled Ideas.

brief autobiography + school daze

Kids and teenagers go to school, and sometimes adults do too.

At school I was dead-popular, a legend some say.

Okay so people who know me, my inner circle, will roll their eyes on reading this cah I talk about it all the time. I mean, like, *all the time.*

It's become a standing joke kind of a thing.

But yes I was a legend and I bask in the glory of this every chance I get, even though I am a full adult now.

I haven't moved on.

I haven't grown up.

I was a County Champion athlete and the top rebel. I hung with the tough kids and was kind of tough myself but mostly I was a crazy fuck.

And my crazy had creativity.

I would do things like set the fire alarms off. Jump out of second storey/story windows into a bush. Fraud free school dinners. Sold stolen bus hammers. We would stop smaller kids from being bullied and this gave us a Robin Hood Effect, which only added to our popularity.

There's tons of other stuff. People still stop me in the street and remind me.

I was the ultimate outlaw, and I enjoyed all the treats which came along with that.

School was the birthplace on my becoming an artist, a storyteller. Soft narcissism but there was too much love in my heart for anything truly bad to happen.

Mostly it was acute attention-seeking.

When I was two year's old I got separated from my parents for six weeks and experts would probably put it down to that.

The need to stand-out and be admired or shock or disgust. Or maybe just the raw pure adrenalin rush of pushing the world to its absolute limits.

Yeah, I like that one.

Of course I am an adult now but I still carry some of that stuff around with me.

Like the first time I saw you in class and I knew you were trouble and troubled but of course that's always been a part of it. Cliché City.

Naughty kids automatically gravitate to the back. Even in the adult world.

They automatically gravitate to each other and test each other out. Who will go the furthest.

Magnets, that draw together, but won't quite

touch

Suppose if I was any kind of poet I'd furnish you and The Reader with full decorative descriptions on what you look like but this ain't that kind of a piece.

It just ain't.

weakendz

School rules:

No Romantic Relationships, section B96 of The Human Conundrum Act.

Not like they didn't know anyway. Not like they didn't know.

You acted so tough at the beginning. Little did I know you'd turn out to be a big ole scaredy cat.

Scaredy pants.

I was 87% sure.

And it's not like they didn't fuckin know anyway.

Acted so bad.
Like you would face anything.
Anyone.

But jus a big ole scaredy cat when it came down to it.

I was 87% sure.
I was 87% sure you were going to block n' bounce once I told you.
87% sure you were gonna drop shoulder once I told you about The Telling.

Cut n' run.

Leave me to it.

Not like they didn't know in the end.
Not. Like. They. Didn't. Fuckin. Know.
They all knew.
Every last one of the beautiful pricks.

We go lie.

Class act. Heads will roll.

Scaredy pants.

I was 87% sure Knew you would. Knew you would but I had to

anyway

Regardless.

Come. Clean.

Not stay dirty. Dingy, tricky.

Not go lie. Not go low.

Dirt man.

Ramshackle. Ragamuffin.

Get out of gutters.

Had to have a rinse and get set straight.

It was about that time.

And it's not like they didn't know anyway.

They *all* knew. And you knew that they knew, too – so what was the point of continuing with the fuckery? Made no sense.

All it did was carry on keeping things shit.
Uphill, hard work, absurd like Sisyphus Rock.
Kind of morbid and mocking, like taking the gee-wiz out of people.

Lack of integrity. *Sheer* lack of personal integrity.

Made us look like pussies is what it did.

Cats. Pants.

Just ole and scaredy.

It was a sad sight to see, I'd say.

No one would work with us. No one would trust us.

And it's not like they didn't know who we are.
The world knows when you're ugly.

So

reverse dem roles now: would you wanna share your deep and personals with someone who go lie

to

yo face?

Would you?
Would you all out there?
Would you all out there, tell it?

Moms and friends and loves and everyone.

Kant and his Moral Law.
His Tango in The Night.

Da trute.

To tell da hole trute and nuthin but, *Jah!*

Aside from that on a purely practical.

On a purely practical, to put the whole class into a fix.
Jam.

Straightjacket. Stranglehold.

Just can't move.
Breathe.

Cah choosing who to work with was a math equation. A series of circuits, dead leads, dead-ends.

Limiting. Unnatural. Rotten.

Wish the word *toxic* hadn't been hijacked otherwise I'd use that one, too.

Two more years of this shit. There's just no way.

In the end.
In the end.

At the weekend when the ends are weak.

It was.

The needs of 15 vs the need of 1.

To make that call.
To fess up and tell it how it is.

Bigger pictures, greater good.

Everything is a representation of something else.

And no one gets away with anything.

In the end.

Act fast act now.

Fore it's too late.

To live your life as if it was being done to yourself.

rationality
rational thinking and rational doing
question shouldn't be how could I, but more how could I not?

raisin reasons

I did not crack, but did it off my own back.

I did it on my own terms, in my own time and for my own reasons.

And don't think it was all *Kumbaya* handholding and instant forgiveness. I took a two-day bad-boy battering on this one. On my own always. Likesay, I had more crimes on me than you. Had much more to face.

That's why the revenge card doesn't work.

Why poke you with a stick and then smash myself with a hammer?

Where the sense in that? Where da *logica* be at?

disciplinary measures

When I was at school I sometimes couldn't do detention cah I would be double-booked with other detentions from other teachers.

When I got suspended me and my mate would come into the school grounds wearing regular clothes (baseball caps and rude boy jackets) and we would stand-out a mile and the attention-seeking thrill we got from this was insane, a total head-rush.

Somewhere along the line I worked out that school always sent letters to my house on a Thursday, so after my Friday morning paper round I would intercept them and take them into class and read them to my fans.

Once the deputy head rang my house and I pretended I was my dad. The second time she did it I got busted.

Now I'm an adult and I'm still getting busted.

So you go truant and I got expelled (almost).

First I had to write a full statement of everything that happen. Then I had to work through a booklet.

In *Kes* the headmaster took them into the office and whipped each palm with a cane.

The best kind of laughter is when you're not allowed to laugh. The funny faces we pull in holding it in. Raw fear mixed with pure joy. Just can't beat it.

I've always liked the word *malfeasance.* Never hear anyone use it but I do, from time to time.

I first heard this word in the great 1996 film, *Fargo.*

cinema

Film. Movies. Pictures.

Popcorn.

I owe my life to cinema.

Yet I have watched nowhere near enough. I am only at the beginning.

I owe my art to cinema, maybe even more than literature.

There are about ten films which live with me constantly and are all over this piece. I would name them but it's important that you don't know where I come from.

Homage is good but mystery is better.

Cinema is what life *could* be if we concentrated more and cared less. If we were more considerate of our moves, and when to pull them.

There is talking and there is dialogue.
I know which I prefer.

For all the haters out there I'll say this – movies are no less real than a mood swing or a bad attitude.

truth or consequences, new mexico

Still there are those who aren't satisfied. They want blood and won't be happy until so. I am hated through the ages. Half a year on and it hasn't tired-out.

"He's swanning about as if nothing's happened."

They hate me.

I'm not repeating myself.
I'm not repeating myself.

other girl

I loved the other girl too.

She saw us tucked into that corner, there. She notices what most miss. She notices almost everything. The corner of her glasses has x-ray vision. Sees right through you. Her rage has past chapters from The History Book. She did the right thing in the wrong way, bit like me, bit like me. I will not repeat myself. I love the other girl. Those small gestures on the big stage. I will not repeat myself.

I blew her up.

I broke her out.

I watched her grow.
I watched her shrink.

I broke her down.

I made her cry.

Made her doubt hersel.
Made her want to smash my skull like a cup. It's a mug's game.

I hurt her head and played with it.
But not like she think.
Not like you say.
I love the other girl too.

capsizin

Even though we in the same boat we kind of wasn't, at the same time. Same time, different boats. Titanic insight. I know this admit this. To as, you and I aren't made the same. Of different stuff. Equipped to handle. Life jackets and willing to throw them out. Less sensitive. Less serious. Less young. Less more, more or less. More ability to concede and get naked in front of the mob. Moby-Dick they couldn't catch him.

amor fati

onslaughts

On onslaughts and admissions, co-confessions. Advise them. Advice here. And not just with this here scene but with all things of this nature.

And that is.

That it is possible to be okay, and be safe in the long run. Shameproof and pain-free. And so to do this all you gotta do relinquish all sense of control and resistance, apply no de-fence whatsoever. Not stick up for yoursel in the slightest but rather just let it all hang out. Bubble-gum. Words wash right through you. An Ego Death, some might say. To be of zero substance as the world attacks you. No identity, almost. Just sacrifice yoursel to the point of invisibility, invincibility. Into. A real warm-womb of swimming oblivion. *Ah.* Just experience it all as if it were a video game or somethin. You can't be scared that way. Can't be a big ole scaredy cat, pants.

But rather a reference point for the future. Just training-ground to toughen-the-fuck-up. Just training-ground for the first Stoic. Losing your self like Zeno losing his cargo for the last time. That day.

This is the moment when a school of philosophy was born.

style of lies

I know we go lie in different ways too. My lie was sweeping and general, technical. Admitting without admitting, like a crim to the fedz without evidence. I was slapdash and showman, cavalier and caveman, comic, nicely topped with presidential parody. Made obvious. I never lied to individual faces, never lied on a real, on a one-to-one. *Ask no questions.* Whereas you lied intimately to persons in full, in private corners. Told big blown stories. Red car.

You drive it into the future.

pour me

an iced tea.

Winter has three months to its name. Just like any other season.

Symmetry is the tool to the cleanliness of memory.

Tip-top. Top tip.

an iced berg.

Was 87%.

Was 87% sure.

Was 87% sure you were going to block when I told you about The Telling.

Big ole.

Big ole.

Prolly framed/justified it yoursel as some sort of grand betrayal.

By the people, to the person.

Vick and Tim are poor people.

Pour you another one.

Scaredy pants.

Some sort of grand betrayal.

To tell the folks back home.

Didn't do nothing wrong on the true double-negative conclusion.

Conscience. Clear.

Your winter intact.

Class act.

back the fuck up

Ethical Framework
climbed it clambered
shat
from
the
t
o
p
s
g
n
i
s
i
Grand R
Normal. Right.

more autobiography

They say they want to see the real me but who is the real anybody? Carl Jung says that we have four or five personas *at least*. I know I do.

I have the serious persona and the comedian persona and the sage persona and the romantic persona and the criminal persona and the artist persona.

The artist persona is my favourite and to be honest I'm really trying to stay in this one most of the time. Hopefully I can *achieve* being in this one *all* of the time. That would be a dream come true.

It's my favourite because it contains a little of all the other personas too.

Here I am free, loving, endless.

everything

It also gets shit done, believe it or not.

Cupid

Limerence gives love a bad name.

Love was there no doubt, but so was limerence so I was pretty much fucked from day dot, from Daycember.

the red book

I gave you my copy of The Red Book. They say don't judge one by the cover of it but this is an exception to the rule. For the outside was just as sublime as the in. A kind of red leather coat with bold gold lettering.

The text was highlighted some so you could have an insight into my insides.

Mostly it talks about 'The Spirit of The Depths,' – where all creativity resides.

rations

From late last summer 'my' rationality was becoming totally insane.

Socrates. Seneca. Spinoza.

All them man-dem.

Nothing got in or out without my say so.

Free, fresh and flowing.

Yet at the same time –

Calm, clean and contained.

Casual. Causal.

Airtight. Alright.

Rationality and well-being is a skillset like anything else. We learn it. We acquire. A gathering of the required tools, to achieve the desired outcome. Like an Olympic athlete in training the wanker philosopher has his training too, his gym, her dojo. Only his colosseum is daily life. To win and lose and sometimes draw. To build and break and sometimes botch.

To track down and go after.

To face *head-on*, and then go back and work it all out. *To think*. To really think *properly* like they did in them olden days, of ancient times. On the steps, of the porch. To balance and weigh opposing forces. Push-pull the pendulum of moments. Events creatively etched into patchwork, needle to thread to sow, the steadiest of hands.

Worlds into worlds we whirl, cycles, circles.

To find

as close to a proven formula as we can possibly get.

The four principles by book: *wisdom, justice, courage, moderation.*

The other favourite of mine, *forbearance*
(that word is funny to me somehow).

Knowledge is the star at the top of the city, holding everything up, overlooking the rest.

The dividing line betwixt dark cave and daylight.

And

the other dividing line betwixt that you can control and that you can't.

Some people know this dichotomy, but a few, if any, actually live it day in/day out.

On this front, in this particular area of expertise, I must humbly say I'm probably the best I know, thus far. Not an overnight ting but a longtime ting. Longtime stay. Lifelong lesson thorough and through. Constant, like glue. Not something one stumbles upon but a thing adhered to.

In short, this shit taketh man time, true.

But the owls are not what they seem.

Cah as toa do, once you think you have it, you don't. Complacency is a killer and always has been. It's an old story. Finds its way home like bone, or a boomerang on loan.

Self-satisfaction soon slips into the stern judge. Turns in on itself.

Made me realise I'm way off the mark of the masters. Not an Epictetus or an Aurelius. Not a black belt but a brown one. Maybe even as low as a purple. *Fuck.*

A thinking thing who simply started to stop one Saturday Night. Wind it down.

Abandoning his post.

Don't you know we do it to ourselves always. In all ways and we can't deny.

No one or nothing does it for us, or *to* us. *We* do it.

Create our state by talking ourselves into realties based on the wants of the time.

You was the want of that time, or someone like you, at least. Slow train coming. The period in question. I could feel it fall in the fall air even before you ever existed.

Stopped my deep reading of *all* things. Took my finger off the pulse.

and by

Opening days of winter Reason was on rest. Standby. Put on ice.
Taking a break. A Siesta called *You.*

pie chart in words

This circle represents a full year. There is a line down the middle, 6 months apiece. On the right side there is a horizonal line halving that, two quarters of the whole, 3 months apiece. In the top quarter is says *up*. And in the bottom quarter it says *down*. On the left half it says *my art*.

So that's –

Dec, Jan, Feb – up.
Mar, Apr, May – down.
Jun, Jul, Aug, Sept, Oct, Nov – my art.

This kind of symmetry happens all the time.
I find it spectacular.

a philosopher's work is never done

The philosopher chillin on the cover of *this* book once said, "all a thinker needs is a quiet room and a rational mind."

The Solitary End.

He once mocked friends of his who showed up at his yard at 11am to find him sitting up in bed, "what are you doing?" they asked, horrified.

"Thinking."

I'm at work *now*, as I type. My mind touching yours with *these words*. Day at the office. Putting a shift in. Graft.

I got my spade and my sledgehammer and rope. Pulling down the Cartesian Crib and rebuilding that baby from scratch.

Pick parts from the whole and turn it slow in the hard light.

A thorough examination, exhumation.

Each part.

Each part that put me there from the start.

These parts which can be broken into smaller parts, sub-parts.

all the way down

Parts which work in isolation and parts which work in combination.

Wot am sayin iz how meny times do da peoples-dem find demsel in states ov mind wivout eva realizin how we gots ere. Hole arenas ov arrivin fort which can be explained by honing-in on da lickle-itty-bitty pieces which took dem dare.

This is what took me to you:

Atmosphere, (*at most fear*)

dust, door, socks, hat, scarf, light, trick, teeth, features, freckles, smoke, mirrors, windows, eyes, stars, air, hair, beauty, brow, alien, musk, mask, scent, sense, senses, sensation, stimulation, simulation, real, risk, dare, thrill, trailblazin, friction, fiction.

Chronology,

timing, time, narrative, memory, palace, map, worlds, words, sentences, books, numbers, dates, lines, lineage, father, daughters, queen, king, philosopher, Christmas, birthday, boy, delivery, birth, future, chance, change, repetition, repetition, reputation, regurgitation, follows, habits.

Minds,

contact, conflict, comfort, convict, newfoundland, likemind, badmind, goodmindgreat, familiar, home, misschief, misstruth, mistake, took, taut, taught, games, give, hopeless, full, flight, vulnurebel, yell, clandestine, destiny, care, career, meta, present, Red Book, Red Pill, sleepish, sweetness, lucidity, dreamy, music.

doubt

muse sick

But music.

But mostly music and that started us off by, and continued with.

maybe you do this all the time

A playlist playing this thing out.

Talking without talking.

Talking through titles.

Starting with *When You Move, I Move* walking us all the way to *Is This Love.* You said that word first.

You did.

After that we on the same sure-footing and paced each other equally. No sudden movements.

Even Flow.

Constant though.

Not a day or a night went by. In each other's lives all the time. Heads. Had our own language and maybe we should have kept it up that way, all the way. Might have been better in the long fun.

Told me what was going on in your headrt with these songs. And I listened to you/them.

But music.

But music is not reliable.

But music is no foundation for a relafriendship to be built on.

Music has its heavenly place we know but there is nothing so anti-reason as music. Lost On You. It swoops and swoons, creates states and sentiment by force. It demands attention. Sets scenes.

Polaroid.
Kaleidoscope.

A mainlining of emotion. Emotion means to *disturb*. A disturber of da peace. That's why those who live and die by music and music alone, are always up and down. Its types are erratic. Inconsistent. At the mercy of adrenalin. Sensualists. Moment-junkies. A five-minute love song. A demo tape passing between slippery hands.

You can't set your watch by them. They cannot be trusted.

"Music makes me lose control."

High on suicide n' Co.

We

wouldn't want to live without of course. Of soul.

Has its heavenly place.

Touches the ethereal but only to be back down again.

reason is the language-ladder to sun, the slow, sure, secret way

Music can realign the cool.
Music takes us out for the night.

But no eternal answers here, no code to fall back on.

What happen when the gig be over and all of the peoples done gone home?

we, us

Music opened us up on. Started us going by. Uneven footing.

Music and Limerence own the same properties. They are intoxicating, undulating bedfellows.

Same could be said for

Your Red Sex

tell me I'm your national anthem
(booyah, baby, bow, down, making me so wow now)

Music is all over this piece.

I to the b

L-Bomb.

Hiroshima.
Her-oshima.

The act of love-bombing.

Hold The Line.

"Toto, I have a feeling we're not in Kansas anymore."

before sunrise

The business of blissfulness. No point to recall cah it don't serve none.

Besides, half of which you choose to forget.

Other half refuse to remember.

cept

for that swedish poet in sweden who came at us from the riverbank.

made you jump. got us started, startled.

"may I ask you a question?" he said.

"yeah," you said.

"so I would like to make a deal with you," he began, pointing at us with five fingers.

"go on," I said, deviating from the script.

"I mean, instead of just asking you for money, I will ask you for a word ... you give me a word ... I take that word and then I will write a poem ... with the word inside ... and if you like it, if you like my poem ... if it adds to your life in any way ... then you can p$y me whatever you feel."

we stepped away at this point at the same time. first word to my head was *milkshake* but first word out of you was *shining*.

you might have been looking at the river.

"shining, okay," he said with a cosmic laugh. "shining it is."

took out his pen and page and turned into the bridge, hunched back over.

once he had written what he had written he read what was about to be said:

"Each man is a half-open door
leading to a room for everyone.

The endless ground under us.

The water is shining among the trees.

The lake is a window into the earth."

handed us his book and sat back down.

at the bottom he wrote something else in your handwriting.

(dated in the corner)

May you stay forever curious . . .
Appreciation Always.

x

the swedish poet gave us permission. he said he was poor but we didn't believe him cos he wore a brand new ted baker scarf and had designer white teeth.

when he moved on he said goodnight and a

lighted ferris wheel turned slow in the way distance, corner of the city.

there's people up there waving one of us said, kissing – can you see them?

not really.

famous muses

Some artists and their famous muses are:

Scott and Zelda Fitz
Jack and Neal Cassady
Virginia and Vita Sackville-West.
Ayn and Lev Bekkerman.
Ted and Sylvia Plath.

I'm not saying we're gonna be famous like those guys but at least we get to fool around a bit.

honeymarooned

The Artist makes a mountain out of a molehill.
The Philosopher a molehill out of a mountain.
The Muse sits on top.

The Other Girl watches on from the corner.

The Reader turns the page.

You roll your eyes.

Columbine blowing bullet-kisses cross class.

Art turns blood into strawberries.
Art makes it all better.

Spring Break forever.

Music is all over this piece.
Cinema too.

Even Time Travel happens in this piece.

It's at this point that everyone is happy.
It was at this point that everyone was

getting their best grades.

Living their best life.

A* students.

A sign of productivity and seemingly settled minds.

If the world just keeps on turning like this.
If we all could just hold it here.

This fork in the road.

A sliding door open, shut.

If we all just hold it.

Everyone.

On a shared mission.

Everything.

We talked about.

Yalom and his Mrs, you said.

If we all just hold our line.

Everyone watches from their corners.

Cah even when you cried, man.

I

come scoop like ice cream.

A Tetris shape.
Loosely locked.

Not going anywhere.

Felt you slowly and silently and supernaturally ground and calm.

Calming. Grounding.

A calm ground.

Everybody watches.
Everybody reads.

If I was a hero in a movie or a hero in a book or a cowboy in a song.

Or if I was just a Real Person in Real Life then I'd say something like,

"Whatever the mess, and whenever the mess gets here, I would be too."

Only a line like that would be ridiculous so I'll get off my horse and keep my mouth

Chaos

girl.

wherever you go it go

This is undoubtedly the most [redacted] chapter of the treatise. The flesh and bones of the piece. Blood and guts. This is where everything be at.

To live your life as if it were being done to yourself.
To treat your life as if it were being done to yourself.

Your bare feet on the cold tiles.

You see my face in your mirror.

Your eyes are my eyes.

So you're in a relationship with man right now, or gyal. You've met body and mind and are loved-up ta fuck. On it. In it. On a real. Everything is easy and of no effort. Got your own language down and everything. Feel safe and at the same time entertained, enthralled. Electric static. He's open with you and you with him. How life should be. How people are really. Future is strong, but not thinking about it too much. Your communication with each other is supple, but there is a very clear pattern which you can call *home*, of growing truth, real honesty. Like your man would tell you if there was anything otherwise. You know where he comes from. A firepower of courage. A preparedness to tweak, should differences meet.

Measured, magnificent. You hold each other well, little by little, day by day. There is form and substance, energy and goodness, not picturesque purity, but *goodness.*

You've both read the books.

Knocking on for three full months your connection has existed now, so you trust this man, somewhat, this lover of yours. Work has been put in, *some* work at least.

You got casual pet-names. You got cute habits. You got plans.

An earned depth, like if there was anything amiss he'd come talk to you direct, or show a sign of invitation.

You send him a gift and he responds with a full-on joyously so.

There is always laughter and not one argument or cross-word yet. No puzzles, no games. Or even the thinnest bones of contention.

Yesterday you got the daily kicks of him calling himself *hubby* and how he's gonna come see you soon, in a few days, yeah. He's on his way to you. A drive on down. Love hearts.

Next day however, bout roast time bout lunch. Sunday. You get an out-the-blue exploding text of panic. Swirling words and spinning heads. Shit has gone down and a tragedy do ensue, an accident or something. Of some kind. Someone he know, a friend, he says. A friend of his and 'their' mother is hysterical. Pronouns. And so is he, your lover, your man. So you hang back and hang strong and hear it out and support still, naturally. All plans and all things go on the backburner and you just listen and be there, give space but be there. That real concern for the other, as is obvious.

Let a day go by, lay of the land.
Next day too, probably.
You keep checking in, minimal, curious, strong.
Wagwan?

Like a bucket of scattered jigsaw pieces but none of them fit, together, yet.
In fact not even *one* got fit, yet.

All you got is a car crash.

You don't know who or how or why or what.

Concerned for your man and his mental state and how he's doing, coping. You want to help, be there, go down to his village but you can't cah he won't. Let you.

A week on touches so now you ask for a phone call cos you have no idea what's going on, happened, in the dark, totally. This is your boy here and you're powerless to be there for him. Only he can't speak cos all he keeps doing is breaking down all the time. Only that is odd cos surely he's having other conversations with mothers and fathers and doctors and hospital peoples and other friends and stuff. Sons. So what can a little 5-minutes harm? And even if the man does break, is that really that bad? Surely the person you need the most at a time like this is your One.

None rings true, to you. You just don't get it, at all.

but the care is on him

You are due to meet and stay with each other for three nights. It's planned and set so you may get some answers now, or a picture of the scene, at least.

Although not quite cos he tells you he can't cos he's needed there.

"I'm needed here."

Not a conversation or explanation but a cutthroat fact of He's Needed There.

This is what you get now and the only thing you get, *I'm needed here.*
You don't know what this means or needed for what but he is needed there.

Eventually you have a word with yourself and fall it back. Obviously something done horrendous has gone happened and this is how he's reacting, dealing with it. Withdrawn, defensive; maybe not used to being loved and supported so you drop shoulder and leave it where it is. Them. People react different to trauma so bigger pictures and all that.

You are not staying with him this weekend.
You are not staying with him cos he's going home cos he's *needed here.*

There.

You see him this weekend but just not staying.

When you do see him he is broken. Says it himself, *broken*. Breaking point and broken, and then some. Doesn't really acknowledge you much but that's only natural cos he's broken.

Only through the day he does start to connect with people, *others*. Slowly, gradually – coming back to life. Fixing. Fixing the broken. Even catch him laughing a few times. You don't stick on this too much cah it's always the nearest who are the furthest away.

Intimacy works that way sometimes, for some people.

No big thing.

That night you go check-in with him and then something happens for the first time.

First time in your three months. A bareback blatant blank. Stark. Never thought you'd become one of them phone freaks but here you are. He's online as we talk and he's blatantly blanking you to your

face.

And the night just goes on and dig and delude and thus and so you don't work it out. Just a dead numbness, you'd say. Senseless and sameness. Of the human race. Movements of youth.

And then mourning more of the same cos you find out that your man didn't go home after all. Not to his village but stayed right here. In your city big. Under your nose.

Lied to you.

The decency of.

You look in the mirror at your own face.
You look out the window at the world.

Slight wind making the trees move.
Making these pages among your fingertips.

We put the book down for a bit and put the kettle on.

Whistle while we wait.

Pick it back up. Take a sip.

Your mind wanders between fiction and Real Life.

It walks a thin line.
It walks the razor edge of this paper.

You start reading again:

Eventually get *some* information.

At last.

Cah you find out that the Car Accident Person isn't a friend but
An Ex.
An Ex that's now a friend. Was.

You find this out second-hand. He told class at the same time he told *you.*

Your lover, your GF, husbandwife.

Facts. Distributing them.

So now something been gleaned.

You wonder why this has been hidden, or not talked about at least.

Shadowy as fuck. Not real not straight-up.

Purposeful, precisely placed behaviour, in this time of

chaos.

You blow on your hot drink to cool it.

A siren whining way in the distance.

Pick up where you left off with a phone call that night and it's a long one. Three hour. A lot is spoken about but not much said. Around the delicate edges. Yes it was An Ex and he didn't want to tell you cos he didn't want you to think there was *anything in it.* To it. How that works you're not entirely sure cah you were going to find out anyway, eventually.

Story is –

was

your mans has stepped in to look after An Ex's kids. There's no one else. You listen and he explains and ultimately you think that is a noble and a good and a beautiful thing to do. You'd do the same and you support it all the way down to the bone. Good like that.

Just be honest with me in the future, you say.

I will, he says.

You're kind of back on track with this phone call. He explains all the shady behaviour and does a good job of it. Mental Health and disorders and used to dealing with things on his

own.

Shows sympathy and sorrow for his –

Just be honest is all I ask, you say.

I will, he says.

he wont

March on.

Spring sprung.

Buds. Warmth.
Spring Break forever.

Still.

Cool. Calm.
Break spring the weather.

Still –

not seen him yet.

In flesh.

Not seen him yet cos he is, still –

needed here.

Just bear with me your patience is –

Thank you. Sorry. Your love is –

Too far away just wait until we –

Breaking point springtime we'll go –

Switzerland. Sweden.

Simmer. Summer.

I'll wear my –

Blue-sky days and a soft yellow dress.

Ankles. Knees.
Not seen him yet but *soon,* soon.

Then

he SUDDENLY tells you that things have taken a turn for the worse, a nasty spill. Again.

Mental Health here, or a lack thereof, reappear.

Chaos.

Chaos back.

Chaos back in –

town. Head.

Don't know what's wrong with me? Happening *to* me? Doctors *for* me, to see my

GP.

And find out what's wrong!

WHATTHEFUCKISWRONG.

I haven't got space. Can't handle anything. Can't handle people.

you

me

So it's here that he ends it with you.

It's here that he ends it with you, *you think.*

Kind of.

Kind of but not really, not all-too clearly.

Mental Health is the reason he gives. Gave. Another 3hr conversation.
Not an easy one, but not really a hard one either. Not too much said, bit of a word salad.

A salad of words.

Here a stone, here a plum, here a grape.

Nowhere you can come home to and wipe your feet on and rest your head.

No carpet, no bed.

When you mention An Ex he goes shifty. Topic change.

Timelines, there are not.
Reasons and exactness, not so much so.

Of course the heart doth breaketh cah you've been spiritually entwined with this individual for the last three months but it's Mental Health and it sounds serious so what's a wigga gonna do??

Just way it is.

It's just –

the way it is *for now.*

He tells you to 'keep in touch.'

Touch and keep.

keep him sweet

Thing is. Thing was.

I know you *gurl* and you're a loyal person, a strong and steadfast individual.

When you in, you in.

For life as such. Life as they say.

Dedicated.

"100% committed."

Thing was. Thing is.

If the signs were gradual and the relationship done lost drive then –

I could understand.

Only

the night before he was calling himsel *hubby,*
signing off with an ILY.

Valentine just days ago and all alright, all light, all bright-and-breezy, not a care in the –

"You. Are. Ridiculous.
And I love it."

Never has your mind known anything so

sudden so sick. Shock

value.

As a Human Being you love him.
As a Human Being you love The Girl
As a Human Being you love the world.

As a Human Being I love you all.

You –

care for this man

kind.

Care for him, so of course not gonna give up on him yet.

Mental Health in reaction to a near-death car crash of a loved one ain't no real evidence to –

throw the towel in yet I mean C'mon I mean –

a hundred people would say the same.

Ask them.

You still my husband, you say, and not abandoning you yet.

He doesn't contest this.

Over the next month there is less and less. Much, much more, of less and less. Slim down and drop fall. Reach out but nothing.

Send birthday through the post but all is flat and nothing.

Nowhere.

You want the truth but doubt you'll get.

Alien.

You want the truth and more than deserve the truth but you doubt you'll get it.

ever

In the end you send a note, the long goodbye.

Cinema all over this.

You not the dramatic kind.
Not the drama type.

Life is life, at the end of the day.

And.

Art is art.

But occasionally the two –

april flowers

Long spring song.

Roll.

Rain running from the top, trickling on d
o
w
n showers

You want the truth but doubt you'll get it.

We've established that.

Big ole scaredy cat.

Doubt you'll get it.

But then you do.

Then you do.

Or a half-hearted stab at it at least, if nothing else.

It comes in the digital post, with bells, with bleeps.

With lights.

Just as you were listening to –

(Don't Fear) The Reaper, Keep Shelly in Athens.

Best cover EVER.

Music is all over this –

You read him.

You read him like a –

He tells you. He shows you.

He tells you something of course – an admission a confession, of sorts.

He tells you.

That the real reason, underlying it all, is, that, there was –

is

the reality is, "my heart belongs to someone else."

Not a big ole scaredy pants after all.

Straight away you unlock and bump back to life.

A ton of bricks.

Someone else.

You had a feeling as such, it checks out ... but not quite.

For the time being tho you don't care and you don't care that you don't care cah –

Just to get the –

Girl in Full.

Your guy back being real.

You can always find out the deets later   you can always, you can

For now you just glad you got that word they learned about in class, *congruence.*

At this news.

At this news I mean most people would lose their shit, but you are not most people.

Alien.

You are

The Artist The Philosopher The Reader The Fool The Humble Pie Baker sayin something like:

"the objective truth is more important than subjective wants and desires."

Yeah that'll do, for now.

You just glad to have his real voice again, not the runaway impostor.

You see him on the other side of the hills.

Stubbled jawline and his good head of hair.

Spanish eyes.

That James Dean t-shirt and his boxing trophies by the bed.

You feel him bolt back to life, too. Happy in himself, new.

I'll always have your back. We are solid.

The things he say.

He reads you a passage from Plato and you laugh and tell him to

just stop hahaha.

Can't help yourself can you, you say.

Transcendent Thinking goin on, he says with electricity, a meeting of minds, *up there.*

Breaking The Norm.

I hope he's alright

Keep on laughing to yoursel.

You. Are. Just.
Ridiculous.

You arrange to meet outside of this book the next day around noonish at the gas station.

You look forward to closure. Look forward to answers.
Mostly.
You look forward to not talking about anything but just catching coffee catching-up.

You look forward to a sentence without a full stop

Period.

At the gas station you kick a stone and wait for him to show. A sign creaks overhead and the dust makes you –

sick, and a bit blind.

You wait for him to show.

You wait for him to turn up.

Only he don't.

Only he won't.

Only he can't.

"He's just fuckin nuts," you shout at the red sky.

Sky don't reply.

He's just fuckin nuts and that's the best explanation you'll get.

And for a few fleeting moments, that explanation gives you all the peace you need.

A fat, soft comforting zero

0

creepin

technically
cheatin officially
but don't care bout that especially now
cos life not black or white angel not myself
in former days especially in raw roaring 20s of
chemicals and pheromoans and typewriters and tripwires
and taunts tricking ourselves by reframing things to make it
fit our own advantages so sympathy for the devil at the end of
the day
night cah people attracted to each other all the time especially
with personality
types like ours of thrill seekers and boat pushers addicted to
fixations and romantical
delusions of movielike sensation swinging moods and cracking
codes broken moral compass
of revolving reloving doors of that much talked about
limerence of yoursours i was telling you
about so go look it up down falling in love while being in love
not your
first time and doubtful last lust probably already moved on
from there two or
three times by now since then hollywood honeymoon on your
period blood
not mentioned age before but here it is and a big factor henry
miller says
wisdom doesn't come with age or with experience as some like
to pretend
but with quickness of spirit sexus another book four you two
read people give us different things at different stages of our
lives like some security some butterlies some wisdom some
intoxication the certainty of uncertainty these long term people

and short term people back from the dead of the future in the city athens platonic i know how it works cah am from around the way like that straight-up philosophy gangsta with a heart o gold spring break forever bitches this aint a bed to lie on but a truth honey bee told from dis muthfuckin art peace

salad

okay okay okay twat i'll tell you the truth don't need to make a whole fucking song and dance about it i mean why not write a book while you're at it don't half like the sound of your own voice don't half like to hear yourself think and do you know how much more of a twat you sound when you say things like *my art* fuck me *my art* give me a break a bucket to be sick in please but okay okay okay i'll tell you the truth in the end if it will help you shut the fuck up and move on up so here hear it is ready steady go so yes my heart belonged/belongs to someone else and that someone else was coma boy yes my ex it's like his near-death crash crush brought him back to life in my arms beating heart so seeing him laying lying here with the grim reaper looming over his almost-corpse vultures a-circlin made me undertake him back so i took him back at the end of life the day it was a simple smooth switch jumping ships from yours to his in the blink of a sigh an ex not an ex anymore not annexed not axed but a flatline waving so happy now so happy now actually actually actually okay okay okay so that's not really rarely the truth at all the truth is was the truth of the truth is that the someone else was in fact indeed a girl the girl or as you say *gyal* yes it was her and it was such a big deal for me at the time a big life choice thing because i needed to stop suppressing the truth of my heart and come-out clean dirty to my parents even tho that don't make sense cos i've never been shy about coming forward never been shy about coming-out even tho bodily i'm as straight as a die queer bob note only theoretically gay for political reasons so i can stand out in the crowd and be counted a part of the struggle minority the majority of me would fuckin revel at the semi-scandal and the attention it would bring fuck all parents burning my village down to a cinder the ground of not letting the bastards grind you down our motto our fathers who art in devon yet yes yalom but i do use sigmund too like he used us back in the day this is payback feud fraud freud sometimes in my work dismantling the men's room urinal with my bare bear glands swollen so there was no girl really if i'm being totally honest honestly i just said that to throw you off the scent sent another red-herring yet again yet another red-herring to keep you on your toes off your balance maybe at the time i thought it would lessen the blow job of masculinity is to not let them think they've lost control aggression yours lurks under the surface like a hungry shark and i was always weary bout that seesaw it with my own step dads buried stoic steps it was born there and i admired that in you not seen it before or since you never allowed it to spill over into the behavioural maybe i was worried for my new now toyfriend because i had consternation that you might revert/resort back forwards to your old style of ways in dealin with things and pay next man a visit blade artist so that's why i said it was a girlfriend we only lasted for a short summer anyway summer of luvin shoving it back in had me a blast while it lasted of the summer wine too old either way the truth is the truth when all said and done that someone else wasn't either coma boy or the girl just someone you didn't don't know someone who i had been communicating with online offline for a while now on-and-off kind of a fling fancy like mad even as i met you luv you last christmas gave you my art but it was getting big bit overwhelming in the knowing too much not enough of my personal needs not my type i like hype not valentine you are ridiculous but five small days later on that saturday night saturday night before i was due to come yours on the sunday i met with this someone else and something happened even tho i didn't intend it to see it cumin shocked me gutted guilted me even tho they narc me title shouldn't use labels to define a soul even tho i do so back to that sat night i sent you 2:11 am text so late it was early telling you i was goin sleep quick in the same bed with this someone else you not the jealous type rare for a man i fell in love with her/him that night that morning i didn't know what to do whit's end winter end soon spring so i waited it out wanted an out needed a reason treason to not come yours a getaway driver to get me out of dodge city sticky situ a white lie wouldn't wash cos i needed a way to get out of it *all* of how to not stay with me next weekend too a way to start the stopping of shutting this shit down *for good* ending things i knew it would be an insane shock to your so nervous system cos we were in our prime at that time centre of honeymoon cementing with trust just needed something big and horrific to destabilase the whole structure of our reality existence as we show it to justify the fall from grace so to the car which did not crash or something like that was what i went with in the end so i sent you that spinning swirling afternoon message late in the day i hope you're following this organised chaos educated madness stylised spiralised chicanery clues codes i did it without thinking mostly mainly manly i wanted to see how much you could take fall like the others soldiers on autopilot like heavy cargo i needed to bring you down through the turbulence runway running away with my expert mouth to give me an out i needed a big scary scene to buy me some time lost on you lost my head so i couldn't be with you haven't got the space for anyone anything little did i know how crazy this would all plan pan out i mean it's obvious now when you think about it i'm telling the truth cos the two states don't even match if you think about it all this dark despair of not being able to talk or eat or sleep yet at the same time managing to cultivate the blossom of a fresh relationship an exciting new connection either way i did feel bad not a monster maybe regardless of what you and the world think did feel awful and there is and was and always will be some *genuine* mental health tissues at play not just crocodile fears but real honest mental health lose it use it to my advantage leverage use it as a weapon shield of gathered chaos of not knowing where to turn and who to turn to even though i only and ever turn to myself at the end of the day i am my own constant constantly pushing people away when it gets too close for comfort forever frightens me like we always said people be people and my name sits bang in the middle of the riddle i know we had a 1000 conversations so why couldn't that just be one of them right friends real i wanted you as a friend to keep you sweet had my career to think about and that transformation but i had to give you the sick silent treatment of spite cos there was no way around it so it was easier to run for the hills and stonewall you to death cos that's what i always do and am used to that by now to do it again and again and still cos bein your bredrin would have meant i would have had to come-out come clean at some point one day and i could never gonna do *that* too scary too naked and anyway universal rule is you can't be friends with exes even tho i don't really classify qualify you as an ex not long enough in the tooth it just doesn't work in my experience and not fair to the new lover in question involved so ultimately that was why the reason for everything is bottle balls bollocks just not having enough of not enough bottle to ride with you and not enough bottle to call it when i couldn't at the time big ole scaredy cat in a nutshell and so to replace bollocks with lies and lies grow into more lies and little lies big love into a life of their own you know that too

you liar yourself gas-lighter so much so we can never turn back
and talkin of lies you kind of lucky too cos if not for the
evidence on your phone i was thinking of playin the whole hole
young girl/older man victim/perpetrator narrative abuse
dynamic card trick treat up my sleeve they would have bought
it too in this day and age i did insinuate it to a few others
circulate that shit sprinkle poison and see how far it travels
across this mind of mine field a whole heap of times but just
imagine if i had think of the route that would have taken us all
too dark to even envisage cave a whole new underworld i
underestimate and don't know about but i'm glad i didn't cos
my soul is rested now and purer for it purer now than it's ever
been truth be told for the first time last time i'm happy really
happy onwards and upwards to the sun of true patient
knowledge ferris wheel we all know and accept chaos now and
how it works like the butterfly effect of ripple to wave to
typhoon the eventual tsunami of chaos this was chaos and it
was touched by all stall and stop breathe take a break me and
breathe me in absorb me so too glad that you the reader have
listened to all i've had to say here life is a picnic salad and i
know you've followed every spoon every drop every word life's
so beautiful it's never gonna end on this never-ending reel real
sentence life art still going long after this book is snapped shut

more on art and muses

Real art, I would say, is trying things which haven't been done before.

Near-impossible, I know.

But it's important to have a go.

Never understand it when they say, his/her art is too self-indulgent.
If you can't play and lose yourself and have a good time in your own art, then when the hell when?

If you can't be a pretentious fuck then what's the point?

Check this:

If only I could translate mind direct to the screen/page then I wouldn't have to write at all. If only you knew what mind saw when I'm not there. When I focus hard focus soft, life is one big eye, one big camera, seeing everything in: close-ups, slow-mo, flashbacks and premonition, long shots wide, underwater birds-eye-view, POV, split screen, dollies, dissolves, reflection, hallucination, animation, neon, noir, phosphorescence – one big dream sequence.

Making cinema is a team sport. *Here* there is just the three of us.

Art is taking pleasure at the half-dressed Santa Claus smashing fuck out of a vending machine.

Chinaman who lives down the road with his two dogs called Silent and Sober.

Muses don't have a reputation for being calm and kind people.
There will be common characteristics which unite them all.

They have their place and purpose.
They stand between that world and this.

Muck into gold, as the moustachioed Superman weakling said.

last scene/seen

Knew, it was to be the last time I saw, you. Wearing sunglasses indoors and the met-her-for of Doc Martens boots. You asked me something outside of The Room, like you were asking a total stranger for directions. *I Don't Know You.* Never seen you before in my life. Depthless contact, surface smile, glacier-eyed.

Just to punctuate my answer with that ridiculous thumbs-up.

You kept forgetting your coat or taking the wrong one, coming back two or three times.

Again and again.

And again.

Coming into being and passing away.

PART TWO

slingin slang

part scholar, part yard man

say –

Mississippi D.A., based on the evidence

Poems

red sex

we all walk the hedonic treadmill
never enough never enough never enough
and she was no so different. more.
but I never followed it like. most.
and that made me diff'rent from the.
rest.

venus flytrap empty eyes porn voice

use me

halloween adult

the faff
I blag

but the
rest I make
magic

love
treats tricks
a shadow knocking on the door

into a classroom
full of other adults
larger than life

taking candy
cracking eggs

the evolution of turtle wisdom

as a kid I thought Michelangelo was the best

twenties, Raph

now Leo

fuck Donatello

future narcissistic weirdo

I've

written so
much clever shit   over the years
that you'd think

I'd

have learnt by now   like

this girl on
the train
who asks
what

I'm

reading?

"Me," I say, closing *this book*

she's staring at
me now the way
you're staring at this

page

People

I AM THE LOVER of.

I love. I am love. There is a force of love.
    I am it.
Don't tell me about love cos I have been around a long time. I know what I'm talking about.

I've been around a long time, even longer than Fear.
I will out-live him easy
I will out-live him in the end.

I will wait him out.

I am better than Fear cos I can get into all the places he can't.

I can be smaller.

Or bigger.

I am not a person.
I am not people.
I am the thing between people.

Your life's work should be learning to accept me.

It's not easy. It's harder than it looks.

You have to be patient.
You will need *will*, and a certain amount of education and style.

But more than anything you'll need bollocks, and the ability to let go.

The ability to say, *yes.*

Maybe you'll need luck.

The more you let me in the more I will spread.

I will work hard for you.
Work hard at making it look easy.
I will make it look natural.

We are at a certain point in history where we are getting good.

You might not think it to look around.
But, we are.

I am not sex.

I am not your bitch.
You are not my man.
Or wife.

I do not pull your hair.
I do not make you burn inside.

This has nothing to do with your favourite position.

Nothing to do with comfort or convenience either.

I am not sex.
I am not *even* making love.

Just love itself.
Just love, man. Straight-up. End of.

I passed you on the street today, remember?

Sometimes I wear a hat.
Sometimes I wear a dress.
Sometimes I wear a tie.
Sometimes I tie my hair up in bunches.

Sometimes I pull a serious face and this just makes you laugh like crazy.

I am the true meaning behind *all* religions.

Most people get it wrong. They either believe in God or they don't believe in God.
But God is the wrong word.
Love is the right word.
Ultimately the problem is a linguistic one.

It's not that complicated.
Simpler than you think.

We just need to cut the shit and go directly to the source.

If you are any kind of thinker then it is your responsibility to lead the way.

Same can be said for warriors and clowns, to some degree.

Night nurse.

I am the love.
Between the people.

I don't have a personality.

I don't have an ego.

I am nothing to do with it.

I am.

I am family.
I am charity.
I am cures.

I am asking you if you're alright.

Or that *exact* moment when an enemy becomes a friend. That surprise on your face.

I am babies.
I am milk.
I am water.

I am sleep.

I don't make mistakes, yet at the same time you need to let me in otherwise we haven't got a fuckin chance.

I don't control everything.
I don't always win.

I am in your hands.

Do with me what you will.

Plath

60
years
to the day
two lifetimes away
she
haunts
this empty
page

Platonic

Two people on stage, a cave, your room. Silhouettes move across the backwall throughout.

ME: I used to know you, didn't I?
YOU: What are all these people looking at?
ME: You, me.
YOU: Uh?
ME: They're here to be entertained.
YOU: What?
ME: It's our job.
YOU: How?
ME: They're here for art, philosophy. Bit of a think. Bit of a laugh.
YOU: Does anybody know what the fuck is going on?
ME: They're here for a bit of happiness. A break from the norm.
YOU: Fuck are these people.
ME: They're here for a bit of friendship. Platform. Tonic. They even named it after him.
YOU: I haven't got time for this.
ME: Pluto. Potato.
YOU: I have enough on my plate.
ME: Smashing. I'll go and get my jacket.
YOU: Haven't got space.
ME: A way for us all to get together. To gather.
YOU: It's not personal I just –
ME: It never is.
YOU: Heard another door close is all.

ME: A serious and good philosopher once said ... that a serious and good philosophical work could be written consisting entirely of jokes.

YOU: I don't find this funny.

ME: It's Bonfire Night.

YOU: It's not even my fault. I didn't do anything wrong.

ME: Right.

YOU: For this I'm not to be blamed in the slightest.

ME: Easy.

YOU: Not as easy as you think.

ME: Writing this.

YOU: Shit I've had to go through to get here.

ME: I can imagine.

YOU: You have no idea.

ME: It came to me in a dream.

YOU: You have no idea but I'm not prepared to go into it right now.

ME: And then the rest just sort of rolls on through.

YOU: I'm at maximum capacity.

ME: There is talking and there is dialogue. I know which I prefer.

YOU: Navigating through some serious shit. Seriously. You have no idea.

ME: Can you hear those fireworks outside, *right now,* up there?

YOU: Breaking point, boiling point.

ME: Above the below.

YOU: Haven't got time. Haven't got space.

ME: Panoramic but you never listened.

YOU: I can't hear rockets, just the dogs barking downstairs.

ME: The Big Italian Delivery.

YOU: Are you writing in future tense, right now?

ME: Past tense, for you.

YOU: Eh?

ME: Multi verse.
YOU: As in lots of words?
ME: I'm typing *these ones* as I go.
YOU: Lying.
ME: In bed.
YOU: For two whole days straight. Night. Love-numb, dumb and half-consciously fake.
ME: Truth thirst.
YOU: I'll face it when I'm ready.
ME: Bed sores.
YOU: I'll tell you when I'm ready, one day promise.
ME: I don't believe a single word –
YOU: Navigating. Capacity. Serious shit.
ME: You say anymore.
YOU: Backed into a corner, I have my escape route.
ME: Of the problem.
YOU: Oh you have no idea.
ME: Lots of them.
YOU: I am a talented singer but nobody knows that. Put my mind to it.
ME: Fear, anger, spite, cruelty.
YOU: In that order?
ME: Occam's Razor: maybe just a wrong-un with an intention to do harm.
YOU: I'm thinking of quitting alcohol.
ME: Evil is underrated, and much more common than we think.
YOU: I won't apologise for my intelligence.
ME: It's in the daily things, mostly. Small slices.
YOU: You don't know the half of it.
ME: I can imagine.
YOU: You have no idea.
ME: *This* doesn't even feel like an idea, as such, it just sort of –
YOU: I am a good persons underneath it all. I paint my friend's

fence. Give clothes to charity. Mindful of pronouns. Help small animals cross the street. Old ladies and retard kids. I contribute to the dying world of real art.

ME: You sound like you're at maximum capacity to me.

YOU: People just don't see.

ME: Is there anything I can get for you, coffee, tea?

YOU: It's them, not me.

ME: A pillow – I mean are you alright?

YOU: I am! I mean, I'm not. Not alright but I am at maximum capacity you're right. Like … if this is a jug (*make a jug-shape with your hands)* and this is the limit of the jug (*pointing your finger)*, well then I'm somewhere around here.

ME: Is that the top?

YOU: Capacity at maximum, yeah.

ME: I'm going to put the kettle on.

YOU: One more drop.

ME: And you'll go over the edge.

YOU: I'll go over the edge definitely.

ME: The edge of the edge.

YOU: Oh you have no idea.

ME: I'm going to put the kettle on.

Pause.

YOU wait for ME to make the tea.

Hear your neighbour taking the stair.

Notice familiar faces in the audience. Your dad's hair.

YOU: I want to go *up there.*

ME: It steams to my left.

YOU: The tea?

ME: I made you a cup.
YOU: One more drop and I'm *done.*
ME: Towel draped to keep the pot hot.
YOU: One more drop and I'm done.
ME: You threw it in.
YOU: Maximum capacity. You have no idea.
ME: You're done.
YOU: I'm done.
ME: And when you're done you're done.
YOU: And when I'm done I'm done. You know this. Anyone will tell you.
ME: Our mothers.
YOU: It's not my fault but if it was I'd tell you because I own my shit.
ME: Say what now?
YOU: I own my shit.
ME: How so?
YOU: I own my own shit.
ME: With whom?
YOU: It's my own shit and it's mine to own.
ME: Say when?
YOU: 1996.
ME: 21st worst Human Being I've ever met.
YOU: Marching orders. Owning corridors. *Achieving* gold. Playground legend.
ME: I didn't think you paid attention at school.
YOU: Sorry, what?
ME: No one was there at the birth.
YOU: Don't talk to me about attention.
ME: No one was there.
YOU: You have no idea by how much little I have.
ME: My father stuffed Christmas presents back up the chimney.
YOU: Your memory is un –

ME: Believable, reliable.
YOU: Class mates.
ME: Da school it got shot up. I remember it well.
YOU: You need to let go of that.
ME: I was 87% sure.
YOU: You need to let go and get a grip.
ME: Which?
YOU: What?
ME: Let go or get a grip?
YOU: We all need to –
ME: Can't do both.
YOU: I just won't –
ME: Can't do both at the same time.
YOU: Curious.
ME: It just doesn't work like that.
YOU: At the same time.
ME: Time. You haven't got any right now, right?
YOU: Right. *Right.* That's what I've been trying to say all along … that, I own my shit but right now I'm at full capacity and can't concentrate for more than a few –
ME: Seconds, minutes.
YOU: *Right.*
ME: Our hours.
YOU: It really is about time you let –
ME: Go.
YOU: Home.
ME: Home time, break time, no time … in the meantime cos time is. Means nothing to me, *for* me. Regarding this. Regarding *all this.* Stick twelve months on but you've still told me nothing. You think time alters externals but it don't.
YOU: The grammar of experience.
ME: For I could write the same thing in a hundred years or more, word for word. Images fresh as a daisy. Dates where

they were. Facts where they are. Memory a house on the hill; a mansion, a palace. Ornaments where they were. Details where they are. Dark. Candle. Blanket. Those Medieval Blues. Dust goes a long way. Staircases sweep to hidden rooms with locked doors – a mind-attic window and the hilly horizon beyond. Windmill. Ocean. Lighthouse. A framed mystery.

Pause.

YOU *look out to the audience.*

YOU: I'd say ... I'd say that most of you are Chaos masquerading as Order ... but maybe the big breakthrough and turnaround is when the opposite is *achieved.*

YOU *drink your tea.*

Pause.

ME: I ... don't know what you're talking about.

Long pause. Actors get up and walk around a bit. Stretch their legs. Sit on a beanbag. Drink from cups.

There are fireworks outside of the cave, the theatre, your room. You close the book up for a moment and listen. A sudden falling silence. Open your eyes, the book.

Start reading again.

YOU: Fuck's happening up there anyway?
ME: Real Life. Real Time.
YOU: Fuck's happening *in here.*

ME: First philosophy. Then art.
YOU: Not this –
ME: Again.
YOU: You're so full of –
ME: Shit.
YOU: Took the words right out of my –
ME: Mouth.
YOU: I'm saying nothing.
ME: The art of philosophy and the philosophy of art.
YOU: Sound of your own –
ME: As she say, philosophy is to clarify what art is to mystify.
YOU: Nobody cares.
ME: The Birth of The True –
YOU: Like I said, when you say that, you sound like a –
ME: Own art attacking me as we speak.
YOU: Twat.
ME: Artist.
YOU: Everybody's gotta learn sometime.
ME: It's humblin really.
YOU: Onslaughts like you said.
ME: Heroically humble.
YOU: Everybody's gotta start somewhere.
ME: Cartesian Crib like I said.
YOU: A kingdom in mind.
ME: Free to construct whatever we want. Against all elements.
YOU: A fortress.
ME: I wouldn't go that far.
YOU: With a torture chamber in the basement.
ME: A simple house will do.
YOU: A door and two windows.
ME: Two eyes and a mouth.
YOU: I don't even talk like this anyway.
ME: What?

YOU: I don't even talk like this.
ME: I never said that you did.
YOU: I don't even talk like this at all.
ME: How do you know *this* is even *you*?
YOU: I don't sound like this. My voice all scratched and stark and slightly common.
ME: I haven't used anyone's name.
YOU: I'm a rare bird and not to be misused.
ME: Not mine not hers not yours not his.

YOU: I'm gonna get this book banned for all that it's worth.
ME: Not much.
YOU: You've got this all wrong.
ME: Ghosts.
YOU: *You've* got *this* all wrong.
ME: Play.
YOU: Failed writer, failed artist.
ME: Failed philosopher, a blip in my career.
YOU: You have no idea.
ME: I have no idea.
YOU: *These* are your words, not mine.
ME: I –
YOU: Shouldn't put them in my mouth.

SOMEONE *says something in the audience, a heckle. Others laugh.*

YOU: See, they're laughing at you. Your failed attempt at love.
ME: Moon. Mountain. Ate a whole wolf in full.
YOU: I have a type. And you're not it.
ME: I'm not one for categorising art but if I *had* to, if I was forced into it then I' d say this is a *prose-poem rap about philosophy and fuck all.*

YOU: You're right about the last bit.

ME: That's what it would say on the front of the tin.

YOU: Dog food.

ME: And on the back of the tin we have the motif of the Ferris Wheel, framed by a circular square of light.

YOU: Papercuts.

ME: Grow on trees.

YOU: Well you're in the palm of mine again aren't you? Coconuts.

ME: Turn me over and take a closer look.

YOU *turn this book over and look at the back.*

YOU: I don't even talk like this.

ME: I've decided, from now on, I'm only going to wear the colours brown and green. Model myself on the form of this –

YOU: Plato frowned upon art, so all you've done is contradict the whole –

ME: Book.

YOU: I never read from cover to cover. Just dip in and out.

ME: Such is –

YOU: My –

ME: Your –

YOU: Life.

ME: Imitates.

YOU: Oh don't even start.

ME: Art keeps the door ajar between dream and –

YOU: I want no part of it.

ME: The unknown.

YOU: I'm known for it.

ME: Art is repetition and symmetry, yet at the same time riding tangents like a wild horse.

YOU: Cliches cover you.

ME: Like a rash?

YOU: I'm itching –

ME: To read –

YOU: People like a book. That's my secret – I get inside people's heads, don't I?

ME: Art is you reading this.

YOU: I'm not reading this.

ME: Yeah you are.

YOU: No I'm not.

ME: I'd say you are.

YOU: I guarantee I'm not.

ME: Looks like it from here.

YOU: You got it wrong this time mister cos I put the book down ages ago and am currently downstairs in the kitchen making an omelette. Washing a dish. At the sink, by the window. Watching an Audi pull out of the close. I'm not in the book or over it. Not holding it. Not reading it. Not *in these* words or *saying these* words.

ME: I bet I can guess what you're gonna say next?

YOU: All this universe, mooniverse, multiverse, multi-dimensional, metaphysical, parallel, panoramic, telepathic, transmigratory, astral, *ad infinitum,* fourth wall, yes-we-too-are-stardust, at-one-with-the-carrier bag is just pure –

ME: Omnipresence.

YOU: Shit.

ME: It gets everywhere don't it?

YOU: All happening at once. Right *now.*

ME: A freckle. An orgasm. A death. A birth. A sneeze. A tornado. A lorry reversing up a snowy street. Your boss. A Bulgarian café in 1973. Mars. This creaking door. The way you say *aunty.* A zebra. A strawberry. The complete works of Shakespeare. Bubonic plague. A 23:59 New Year's voicenote as the digits doth flip. Click of a radiator. Crack in a mirror. A dimple. A thumb. A moonless midnight. Coffee on the rocks. Socks. The Wages of Sin. Age of Enlightenment.

YOU: I get the picture.

ME: Dorian Gray. Salt. A soggy sandcastle crushed under foot. A wave goes in, a wave goes out. One takes its first breath while one takes its last. Athens. August. The room. Sixteen candles blown out in the year 2096. A paperclip. DNA. This book, this sentence, this *word* ... now whisk all that up into a smooth paste, crack in a few eggs, sprinkle a bit of cheese, stick a cherry on top and then pop it in the freezer until Armageddon.

YOU: It's all breaking up.

ME: Breaking down.

YOU: Breaking through.

ME: Bet I can guess what you're gonna say next?

YOU: You haven't got a leg to stand on.

ME: Bet I know what you're going to say?

YOU: Say what?

ME: You're gonna say –

YOU: I'm not here for your amusement.

ME: See. I knew it. Just knew you were gonna say *that very line*, at a time like this.

YOU: But it's true cos I'm not. Not here for your amusement cos I'm not a muse. Not *your* muse or his muse or anybody else's. Muse. Truth be told I'm a fully-formed individual human being with my own voice and brain and mind and soul and heart and lungs and fingers and toes. Not amused and don't find it amusing that you think I'm your muse. Not a muse, not a mute, not your flute. Not to be played. I object to being an object. Not your portrait, your portal, your petal. I'm not a flower to be plucked. I'm not to be fucked about. You see. You say. Do you see what I'm saying?

ME: I know you're not playing. I know.
YOU: I am not here for other people's entertainment.

Pause.

ME: I am.

A slow round of applause begins to ripple through the audience. Louder, louder – until standing ovation.

I walk forward and bow, humbly.

A whistle. A scream. A bouquet of flowers.

After the applause people begin to leave, a steady single file stream.

You look around, confused. Blinking at the blinding sunlight, which strobes intermittently through the clapping fire door way at the back, high up.

You shake your head and take centre stage.

YOU: Where are you all going? Why are you all leaving? There's still people reading this, *on the other side*. People still *here* so I'll continue ... continue to perform ... we don't need you anyway. I don't need you. I'll carry on regardless. Although I'm not one for monologues. Attention. I'm not one to be at the centre of it. Really not one for monologues so I'll keep this short and sweet. I just came here to drink tea and relax. Read a book in peace. Not *this* book but a good book. The right book and not the wrong one. I am a reader when all said and done. *The* Reader. I mean I am a part of this am I not? You can even check me out on the cast credits. I'm here. There is a place for me. The Reader.

The reader reading. That's what we do. Without me you are nothing. Without me this book wouldn't *even* exist. It wouldn't be written. It wouldn't be opened cos there would be nothing inside. Without me the walls would crumble and the words would starve. I am bums on seats. I am the ears of a nation. The voice of the unborn. I don't even talk like this anyway. I don't even talk like this. Not one bit. I'm not to be blamed in the slightest. I just like to dip in and out every once in a while. Live on my instincts and do what feels right at the time. Do something significant with my life before turning 30, 50. Before I'm dead at least. See I'm all about learning. All about learning but they took that away from me. I was never meant for school or any form of formal education cos my mind is too *out there.* Up here. I am The Reader and I don't just read books. I read – faces, hands, hearts, heads. I read situations. I read the room. I read the wind. Read nature. These boots are made for reading. I'll be the reader way after these words run out and the book is closed. *Your* book is only the tiniest tip of the largest ice berg. You are small fry. Big fish in a small library. You don't know the half of it. You have no idea. I am The Reader and I don't mind having multiple books on the go. At the same time. Worlds are everywhere. Words are like open wounds, to me. I float through them like Orlando and Leopold Bloom and Huck Finn, like Holden Caulfield and Sal Paradise and Jane Eyre. Like Daisy Buchanan. I'm not one to name-drop because I keep myself humble at all times. Humble like the writer of *this* book. All artists are covert control freaks and all readers are overt masochists. *Use me.* And let me finish what I'm saying cos I'm not one for monologues. So just let me formally introduce myself before I go, and before he starts with his bullshit again. Right well I am just your average reader as said. The Reader. Sometimes I am a boy and sometimes I am a girl. Sometimes I am gay and sometimes I am straight. My skin is colourless and

I'm a person of indeterminate height. Once I was fat and the time before that way too thin. Now I'm just about right, whatever that means. Overall I don't understand this book but at least I understand life. I am getting there anyway. I have friends but not enough and really I should get rid of some and just have the right ones. One day I will really break out and be the person they don't want me to be. A real rebel with a heart of gold. One day you will close this book and stop reading me between your lines. Connect with the real me in Real Life. Yes, I'd like that. I'd like that a lot. We can have an easy afternoon of coffee and cake. A walk in the park. You can tell me all about your life and I'll listen attentively. To. Every. Single. Word. You. Have. To. Say.

Pause.

ME: Nice monologue.
YOU: *Your* monologue.
ME: Where did you learn to write like that?
YOU: Didn't. Listen. To. A. Single. Word. I. Said. Did you?
ME: Can you believe I'm gonna finish writing this on my birthday. On my birthday *exact.* I mean what are the chances??
YOU: Timing is everything.
ME: People don't end, they just become an example. Archetype. Algorithm.
YOU: Why can't you talk normal? Instead of basing your *entire* personality on trying to impress people.
ME: I'm –
YOU: Losing track on who is saying what? Is this me talking now or is it you?
ME: Highest reason and deepest instinct form the same circle. Holding everything inside.
YOU: That was you. I'd never say shit like that.

ME: What about this?
YOU: So I am you and you are me?
ME: It's all the same bag of bones anyway.
YOU: Yup.
ME: Yep.

A dark wind has been blowing through all this. Making its pages howl.

YOU: Well, I hate to be a killjoy but I think we should really start looking at ... *wrapping this thing up.*
ME: Oh, I was just getting warmed-up.
YOU: People have homes to go to.
ME: They're already in them, *look.*

The page shines into a mirror for a moment.

YOU: C'mon.
ME: But I got a few more lines left.
YOU: No.
ME: Wisdom for the road.
YOU:

YOU *don't answer. An uncomfortable silence instead.*

YOU: Happy Birthday anyway.
ME: Thank You.
YOU: Was gonna buy you a good book but couldn't find one.
ME: **Clearly insane knows nothing so sane and clear.**
YOU: Eh?
ME: Daughters of Necessity on The River of Neglect.
YOU: What's that?
ME: Just getting those final lines in before I bounce.
YOU: Oh.

ME: Father of sons, fathering fathers.
YOU: Done?
ME: Wait, one more.
YOU: Fucksake.
ME: To quote Melville, "Real strength never impairs beauty or harmony, but it often bestows it, and in everything imposingly beautiful, strength has much to do with the magic."
YOU: Now are we done?
ME: Yep. I'm all out. We good to go.
YOU: Thank God for that.

I nod, accept, relax.

YOU: So I just, simply, close *this* up.
ME: Just close it up, yeah.
YOU: And then what?
ME: And then nothing.
YOU: You mean just close it like this, with a quick clap of the hands?
ME: Yes just like that, decisive, sudden, perfect. Ceremonial.

YOU *roll your eyes.*

And then do just that –

Clap this shit shut so hard it makes a sound.

YOU *look around the room.*

Then down at the book.

And the book looks back.

Ingram Content Group UK Ltd.
Milton Keynes UK
UKHW040648290323
419341UK00003B/82

9 781789 633665